MW00435706

THOREAU ON NATURE

Thoreau on Nature

Sage Words on Finding Harmony with the Natural World

Henry David Thoreau

Introduction by
Nick Lyons

Skyhorse Publishing

Skyhorse Publishing books may be purchased in bulk at special discounts for sales promotion, corporate gifts, fund-raising, or educational purposes. Special editions can also be created to specifications. For details, contact the Special Sales Department, Skyhorse Publishing, 307 West 36th Street, 11th Floor, New York, NY 10018 or info@skyhorsepublishing.com.

Skyhorse® and Skyhorse Publishing® are registered trademarks of Skyhorse Publishing, Inc.®, a Delaware corporation.

Visit our website at www.skyhorsepublishing.com.

10 9 8 7 6 5 4 3 2 1

Library of Congress Cataloging-in-Publication Data is available on file.

Cover designer: Jane Sheppard

Print ISBN: 978-1-63450-461-4
Ebook ISBN: 978-1-63450-478-2

Printed in the United States of America

CONTENTS

INTRODUCTION

"A WORD FOR NATURE"

"I wish to speak a word for Nature," Thoreau begins his fine essay "Walking"—and adds, "for absolute freedom and wildness." He did so, with passion and vision, in his important books, his essays and talks, and in the thousands of pages of journal entries that posthumously yielded a trove of brilliant unpublished prose.

Thoreau's ideas about our relationship with the natural world, written more than one hundred and fifty years ago, have never been more valuable to our lives than they are today. He never advises that we build a cabin in the woods and live alone, as he did for a time. But every word he wrote reminds us to make our lives and our understanding much closer to the natural world and to protect our environment whenever possible.

He is remembered today for his firm commitment to civil disobedience as a response to governments that his conscience told him were immoral in some central respect, and for his uncompromising stands against slavery, against Northern lassitude and compliance with the Fugitive Slave Law, and in defense of John Brown. But mostly we remember his lifelong devotion—as one of its seminal advocates and most memorable spokesmen—to the natural world. In his two books, *A Week on the Concord and Merrimack Rivers* and his classic *Walden* and essays like "Walking," he lived by his fierce belief that "in wildness is the preservation of the world," a phrase that now stands as one of our most iconic conservation maxims.

Henry David Thoreau was born in Concord, Massachusetts, in 1817, and died in Concord in 1862 at the age of forty-four of tuberculosis. Franklin Sanborn described him as "a little under size, with a huge Emersonian nose, bluish grey eyes, brown hair, and a ruddy weatherbeaten face, which reminds me of some shrewd and honest animal's—some retired philosophical woodchuck or magnanimous fox. . . . He walks with a brisk, rustic air, and never seems tired." He trusted that his corner of the state contained all he needed to know and he explored it minutely, traveling only intermittently and for brief periods to Staten Island to tutor relatives of Emerson, to Eagleswood, New Jersey, where he met Walt Whitman, whom he admired greatly, and to Canada and Maine. "Two or three hours' walking," he said, "will carry me to as strange a country as I expect ever to see." Early on, he was fortunate to meet his Concord neighbor: Ralph Waldo Emerson, fourteen years his senior, whose family Thoreau would live with as a caretaker for a time.

Much of Thoreau's vision had its roots in the Emersonian concept of "self reliance" and Transcendentalism, and his cabin at Walden Pond was actually built on land owned by Emerson. The two men remained friends until Thoreau's death—though they quarreled at times—and Emerson's eulogy and eventual essay on Thoreau is the best contemporary view we have of the man.

Like Wordsworth, who also influenced his thinking, Thoreau believed from an early age that "getting and spending we lay waste our powers," and that consequently, "Nothing we see in Nature that is ours." He deplored the despoilers of nature—those who destroyed land, forests, or fauna for profit, like the gold-miners who left the world "cut up with foul pits," but also those who diminished their own vital life by commerce. All trade, for him, led down. He had distinguished himself only modestly at Harvard and after graduating he taught school briefly, founded (with his older brother John) a short-lived school of their own, worked sporadically in his father's pencil factory, surveyed land, provided specimens to Harvard, became a skilled woodworker. In Emerson's words, he also showed "a natural skill for mensuration," or measuring distances, depths of ponds and rivers, and the heights of mountains.

His philosophy, so vibrantly stated in *Walden*, was that a man is rich in proportion to the number of things he can afford to leave alone. "Simplify, simplify, simplify," he said. "Let your affairs be as two or three, and not a hundred or a thousand." Thoreau lived this to the extreme. Emerson recalled that few "lives contain so many renunciations. He was bred to no profession; he lived alone; he never went to church; he never voted; he refused to pay a tax to the State; he ate no flesh, drank no wine, he never knew the use of tobacco; and, though a naturalist, used neither trap nor gun." Thoreau needed little enough to sustain him. He once said, "I have a faint recollection of pleasure derived from smoking dried lily-stems," and had "never smoked anything more noxious." A crowded life drew people away from the natural world and Thoreau judged the failures of a life by the degree to which it departed from the ways of Nature.

By 1845, when Thoreau went to build himself a cabin and live mostly at Walden Pond, he was prepared to write his remarkable second chapter in *Walden,* "Where I Lived and What I Lived For." It presents the clearest exposition of the principles that animated his sojourn to the pond—and his life—and is worth quoting at length. "I went to the woods because I wished to live deliberately, to front only the essential facts of life, and see if I could not learn what it had to teach, and not, when I came to die, discover that I had not lived. I did not wish to live what was not life, living is so dear; nor did I wish to practise resignation, unless it was quite necessary. I wanted to live deep and suck out all the marrow of life, to live so sturdily and Spartan-like as to put to rout all that was not life, to cut a broad swath and shave close, to drive life into a corner, and reduce it to its lowest terms, and, if it proved to be mean, why then to get the whole and genuine meanness of it, and publish its meanness to the world; or if it were sublime, to know it by experience, and be able to give a true account of it in my next excursion."

He did not succeed, in the world's terms, during his lifetime. He paid for the publication of *A Week on the Concord and Merrimack*

Rivers and after only about three hundred copies sold, the publisher sent him the remaining seven hundred, which led Thoreau to quip that he had a library of one thousand books, seven hundred of which he had written himself. Even *Walden* sold a scant two thousand copies. But his diamond-sharp prose cast a pure light that shines brighter now than ever, one that the world, faced with such threats as climate change, fracking, and the extinction of more and more species and wilderness, needs sorely. His concept of non-violent protest inspired Gandhi and Martin Luther King, Jr., and thousands of others. John Muir, John Burroughs, the Sierra Club, Edward Abbey, Bill McKibben, Edward Hoagland, John Graves (especially in *Goodbye to a River*), and others have followed his light and have advanced our love and understanding of the beauty and power of Nature.

Like Emerson, Thoreau is eminently quotable. This modest basket of spirited and memorable words about nature offers a valuable introduction to the man and his ideas about life and how to live it. Thoughtfully collected by Erica Gordon-Mallin, who has divided them into seven helpful sections, these quotes explore the links between nature and health, happiness, work, spirituality, priorities, and human relations. Hopefully, these words will lead you to his major writings, where his ideas are expressed in greater detail.

Thoreau's "word for Nature"—its freedom, its wildness, and its capacity to open our minds and inspire in so many ways—has rarely been equaled. The quotations in this book help us to feel the force of his vision.

—Nick Lyons

THOREAU ON
NATURE

Chapter 1

BODY AND SOIL

Thoreau's Spartan habits and thoughtful attention to his health could not ultimately keep him from succumbing early to the tuberculosis endemic to his family, from which John, his older brother, died young. But no one tried harder. By living with care and conscientiousness, he aimed to keep his body healthy so that he could concentrate on his higher thoughts. His life was eminently balanced—from the natural exercise he took every day, to his life close to the soil, to the food and drink he needed to sustain himself.

Water was his preferred beverage and he called it "the only drink for a wise man." He rose early, loved walking, preferred manual work, and ate mostly what we would call "organic" vegetables—beans, potatoes, corn, peas, and turnips that he raised himself. "It was fit," he says in *Walden*, "that I should live on rice mainly, who loved so well the philosophy of India." He made his own bread, of Indian meal and salt, mixed with rye. And of course he walked and walked and was so fit that he was never known to get tired. He especially admired the life of American Indians and in ways patterned his life on what he saw as the essential health of their ways. Thoreau's last words were reportedly "Moose. Indians."

I was not designed to be forced. I will breathe after my own fashion. Let us see who is the strongest.

I am glad to have drunk water so long, for the same reason that I prefer the natural sky to an opium-eater's heaven.

Live in each season as it passes; breathe the air, drink the drink, taste the fruit, and resign yourself to the influences of each. Let them be your only diet drink and botanical medicines.

I am alarmed when it happens that I have walked a mile into the woods bodily, without getting there in spirit.

What is called genius is the abundance of life and health.

Man wanted a home, a place for warmth, or comfort, first of physical warmth, then the warmth of the affections.

Comparatively, tattooing is not the hideous custom which it is called. It is not barbarous merely because the printing is skin-deep and unalterable.

Nature is as well adapted to our weakness as to our strength.

You must love the crust of the earth on which you dwell more than the sweet crust of any bread or cake. You must be able to extract nutriment out of a sand-heap. You must have so good an appetite as this, else you will live in vain.

I have found it to be the most serious objection to coarse labors long continued, that they compelled me to eat and drink coarsely also.

Sometimes we are clarified and calmed healthily, as we never were before in our lives, not by an opiate, but by some unconscious obedience to the all-just laws, so that we become like a still lake of purest crystal and without an effort our depths are revealed to ourselves.

We must learn to reawaken and keep ourselves awake, not by mechanical aid, but by an infinite expectation of the dawn.

Every man is the builder of a temple, called his body, to the god he worships, after a style purely his own, nor can he get off by hammering marble instead.

We need pray for no higher heaven than the pure senses can furnish, a *purely* sensuous life. Our present senses are but the rudiments of what they are destined to become. We are comparatively deaf and dumb and blind, and without smell or taste or feeling.

I believe that water is the only drink for a wise man; wine is not so noble a liquor; and think of dashing the hopes of a morning with a cup of warm coffee, or of an evening with a dish of tea! Ah, how low I fall when I am tempted by them!

He who distinguishes the true savor of his food can never be a glutton; he who does cannot be otherwise. . . . Not that food which entereth into the mouth defileth a man, but the appetite with which it is eaten. It is neither the quality nor the quantity but the devotion to sensual savors.

Every generation makes the discovery that its divine vigor has been dissipated, and each sense and faculty misapplied and debauched. The ears were not made not for such trivial uses as men are wont to suppose, but to hear celestial sounds. The eyes are not made for such groveling uses as they are now put to and worn out by, but to behold beauty now invisible.

I can easily walk ten, fifteen, twenty, any number of miles, commencing at my own door, without going by any house, without crossing a road except where the fox and the mink do. First along by the river, and then the brook, and then the meadow and the woodside. There are square miles in my vicinity which have no inhabitant. From many a hill I can see civilization and the abodes of man afar. The farmers and their works are scarcely more obvious than woodchucks and their burrows.

Any nobleness begins at once to refine a man's features, any meanness or sensuality to imbrute him.

I have found it to be the most serious objection to coarse labors long continued, that they compelled me to eat and drink coarsely also.

I have heard of a man lost in the woods and dying of famine and exhaustion at the foot of a tree, whose loneliness was relieved by the grotesque visions with which, owing to bodily weakness, his diseased imagination surrounded him, and which he believed to be real. So also, owing to body and mental health and strength, we may be continually cheered by a like but more normal and natural society, and come to know that we are never alone.

We must go out and re-ally ourselves to Nature every day. We must make root, send out some little fibre at least, even every winter day. I am sensible that I am imbibing health when I open my mouth to the wind. Staying in the house breeds a sort of insanity always. Every house is in this sense a hospital. A night and a forenoon is as much confinement to those wards as I can stand. I am aware that I recover some sanity which

I had lost almost the instant that I come abroad.

All health and success does me good, however far off and withdrawn it may appear; all disease and failure helps to make me sad and does me evil, however much sympathy it may have with me or I with it.

I was not designed to be forced. I will breathe after my own fashion. Let us see who is the strongest. Every man is the builder of a temple, called his body, to the god he worships, after a style purely his own, nor can he get off by hammering marble instead. We are all sculptors and painters, and our material is our own flesh and blood and bones.

Chapter 2

REAPING REWARDS

Thoreau greatly admired the value of work—but not all work. He remained an enemy of most commerce and decried work that demeaned the worker or wrecked havoc on the earth. In his powerful essay "Life without Principle," he states firmly that "The ways by which you may get money almost without exception lead downward." After he read a vivid, detailed account of gold-digging in Australia, not only did he deplore that the land for more than thirty miles was suddenly "honey-combed by the pits of miners," but he also called the gold-digger "the enemy of the honest laborer," more closely to be compared to a gambler than to a plowman. The gold obtained may have come from hard work but "So does the Devil work hard."

What is the result of the work, he always asks—what is the reward? "A grain of gold," he says, "will gild a great surface, but not so much as a grain of wisdom." He admired hard labor in a field because it could add to the beauty and value of the land but also because in itself it added to the character of the laborer.

The reward of work lay in the work itself, then, and how it was performed. But also important were its actual results. Part of the great "work" he did at Walden Pond was physical—the satisfaction of building the cabin he lived in, growing the food he ate— but a good part was "working" on how he thought and what he learned. Minute observation was work. Thinking was work. One of the rewards, clearly, was *Walden*.

It is not enough to be busy. So are the ants. The question is: What are we busy about?

This world is a place of business. What an infinite bustle! I am awaked almost every night by the panting of the locomotive. It interrupts my dreams. There is no sabbath. It would be glorious to see mankind at leisure for once. It is nothing but work, work, work. I cannot easily buy a blank-book to write thoughts in; they are commonly ruled for dollars and cents. An Irishman, seeing me making a minute in the fields, took it for granted that I was calculating my wages. If a man was tossed out of a window when an infant, and so made a cripple for life, or scared out of his wits by the Indians, it is regretted chiefly because he was thus incapacitated for—business! I think that there is nothing, not even crime, more opposed to poetry, to philosophy, ay, to life itself, than this incessant business.

But lo! men have become the tools of their tools.

In my opinion, the sun was made to light worthier toil than this.

Most are engaged in business the greater part of their lives, because the soul abhors a vacuum and they have not discovered any continuous employment for man's nobler faculties.

A man is rich in proportion to the number of things he can afford to let alone.

Men will lie on their backs, talking about the fall of man, and never make an effort to get up.

Men think that it is essential that the Nation have commerce, and export ice, and talk through a telegraph, and ride thirty miles an hour, without a doubt, whether they do or not; but whether we should live like baboons or like men, is a little uncertain. If we do not get out sleepers (railroad ties), and forge rails, and devote days and nights to the work, but go to tinkering upon our lives to improve them, who will build railroads? And if railroads are not built, how shall we get to heaven in season? But if we stay at home and mind our business, who will want railroads? We do not ride on the railroad; it rides upon us. Did you ever think what those sleepers are that underlie the railroad? Each one is a man, an Irishman, or a Yankee man. The rails are laid on them, and they are covered with sand, and the cars run smoothly over them. They are sound sleepers, I assure you. And every few years a new lot is laid down and run over; so that, if some have the pleasure of riding on a rail, others have the misfortune to be ridden upon. And when they run over a man that is walking in his sleep, a supernumerary sleeper in the wrong position, and wake him up, they suddenly stop the cars, and make a hue and cry about it, as if this were an exception. I am glad to know that it takes a gang of men for every five miles to keep the sleepers down and level in their beds as it is, for this is a sign that they may sometime get up again.

Be true to your work, your word, and your friend.

What is once well done is done forever.

As for doing good; that is one of the professions which is full. Moreover I have tried it fairly and, strange as it may seem, am satisfied that it does not agree with my constitution.

So behave that the odor of your actions may enhance the general sweetness of the atmosphere, that when we behold or scent a flower, we may not be reminded how inconsistent your deeds are with it; for all odor is but one form of advertisement of a moral quality, and if fair actions had not been performed, the lily would not smell sweet. The foul slime stands for the sloth and vice of man, the decay of humanity; the fragrant flower that springs from it, for the purity and courage which are immortal.

Do not be too moral. You may cheat yourself out of much life. Aim above morality. Be not simply good; be good for something.

What you get by achieving your goals is not as important as what you become by achieving your goals.

Only he is successful in his business who makes that pursuit which affords him the highest pleasure to sustain him.

Live your beliefs and you can turn the world around.

Let us spend one day as deliberately as Nature.

Behave so the aroma of your actions may enhance the general sweetness of the atmosphere.

To affect the quality of the day, that is the highest of arts.

If you have built castles in the air, your work need not be lost; that is where they should be. Now put the foundation under them.

We are not what we are, nor do we treat or esteem each other for such, but for what we are capable of being.

Men have an indistinct notion that if they keep up this activity of joint stocks and spades long enough all at length will ride somewhere, in next to no time, and for nothing; but though a crowd rushes to the depot, and the conductor shouts "All aboard!" when the smoke is blown away and the vapor condensed, it will be perceived that a few are riding, but the rest are run over, —and it will be called, and will be, "A melancholy accident." No doubt they can ride at last who shall have earned their fare, that is, if they survive so long, but they will probably have lost their elasticity and desire to travel by that time. This spending of the best part of one's life earning money in order to enjoy questionable liberty during the least valuable part of it, reminds me of the Englishman who went to India to make a fortune first, in order that he might return to England and live the life of a poet. He should have gone up garret at once. "What!" exclaim a million Irishmen starting up from all the shanties in the land, "is not this railroad which we have built a good thing?" Yes, I answer, comparatively good, that is, you might have done worse; but I wish, as you are brothers of mine, that you could have spent your time better than digging in this dirt.

Why should we live with such hurry and waste of life? We are determined to be starved before we are hungry. Men say that a stitch in time saves nine, and so they take a thousand stitches today to save nine tomorrow.

I see young men, my townsmen, whose misfortune it is to have inherited farms, houses, barns, cattle, and farming tools; for these are more easily acquired than got rid of. Better if they had been born in the open pasture and suckled by a wolf, that they might have seen with clearer eyes what field they were called to labor in. Who made them serfs of the soil? Why should they eat their sixty acres, when man is condemned to eat only his peck of dirt? Why should they begin digging their graves as soon as they are born? They have got to live a man's life, pushing all these things before them, and get on as well as they can.

A man may be very industrious, and yet not spend his time well. There is no more fatal blunderer than he who consumes the greater part of life getting his living.

Most men, even in this comparatively free economy, through mere ignorance and mistake, are so occupied with the factitious cares and superfluously coarse labors of life that its finer fruits cannot be plucked by them. Their fingers, from excessive toil, are too clumsy and tremble too much for that.

The laboring man has not leisure for a true integrity day by day; he cannot afford to sustain the manliest relations to men; his labor would be depreciated in the market. He has no time to be any thing but a machine. How can he remember well his ignorance—which his growth requires—who has so often to use his knowledge?

Chapter 3

SEASONS CHANGE

In cities it is possible to miss the full drama of the changing seasons. There is the cold and inconvenience of snow in the winter— where snow in hours turns grey, then black; spring brings some relief and the days grow longer; there are the blistering days of summer, when the heat is heavy and wet; and fall is a time to feel that summer has passed and hopefully winter will not start in November.

The seasons are dramatically different for Thoreau. The first moments of spring bring the breaking up of the ice on Walden Pond, and Thoreau meticulously charts its temperature and the minute changes in land and fauna—the way bubbles in the ice operate as burning glasses to melt the ice beneath. He hears the blue-bird, song-sparrow, and red-wing; he watches how sand flows in the thaw and sees the regeneration of golden-rods, pinweeds, johns-wort, cattails. And then there is the first sparrow of spring.

All the seasons, for Thoreau, have their discrete and halcyon moments, colors, and images. Living close to the earth, his eyes and brain alert, he sees them and knows their names.

The dry grasses are not dead for me. A beautiful form has as much life at one season as another.

Nature now, like an athlete, begins to strip herself in earnest for her contest with her great antagonist Winter. In the bare trees and twigs what a display of muscle.

Summer is gone with all its infinite wealth, and still nature is genial to man. Though he no longer bathes in the stream, or reclines on the bank, or plucks berries on the hills, still he beholds the same inaccessible beauty around him.

Is not January the hardest month to get through? When you have weathered that, you get into the gulfstream of winter, nearer the shores of spring.

Why do you flee so soon, sir, to the theaters, lecture-rooms, and museums of the city? If you will stay here awhile I will promise you strange sights. You shall walk on water; all these brooks and rivers and ponds shall be your highway. You shall see the whole earth covered a foot or more deep with purest white crystals . . . and all the trees and stubble glittering in icy arm.

We discover a new world every time that we see the earth after it has been covered for a season with snow.

To him whom contemplates a trait of natural beauty, no harm nor despair can come. The doctrines of despair, spiritual or political servitude, were never taught by those who shared the serenity of Nature. For each phase of Nature, though not invisible, is yet not too distinct or obtrusive. It is there to be found when we look for it, but not too demanding of our attention.

Things do not change; we change.

Every generation laughs at the old fashions, but follows religiously the new.

I cannot make my days longer so I strive to make them better.

Time is but the stream I go a-fishing in. I drink at it; but while I drink I see the sandy bottom and detect how shallow it is. Its thin current slides away, but eternity remains.

The youth gets together his materials to build a bridge to the moon, or, perchance, a palace or temple on the earth, and, at length, the middle-aged man concludes to build a wood-shed with them.

The price of anything is the amount of life you exchange for it.

Perhaps we should never procure a new suit, however ragged or dirty the old, until we have so conducted or enterprised or sailed in some way, that we feel like new men in the old, and that to retain it would be like keeping new wine in old bottles.

Sometimes, in a summer morning, having taken my accustomed bath, I sat in my sunny doorway from sunrise till noon, rapt in a revery, amidst the pines and hickories and sumachs, in undisturbed solitude and stillness, while the birds sing around or flitted noiseless through the house, until by the sun falling in at my west window, or the noise of some traveller's wagon on the distant highway, I was reminded of the lapse of time. I grew in those seasons like corn in the night, and they were far better than any work of the hands would have been. They were not time subtracted from my life, but so much over and above my usual allowance. I realized what the Orientals mean by contemplation and the forsaking of works. For the most part, I minded not how the hours went. The day advanced as if to light some work of mine; it was morning, and lo, now it is evening, and nothing memorable is accomplished.

Not till June can the grass be said to be waving in the fields. When the frogs dream and and the grass waves and the buttercups toss their heads and the heat disposes to bathe in the ponds and streams, then is summer begun.

In any weather, at any hour of the day or night, I have been anxious to improve the nick of time, and notch it on my stick too; to stand on the meeting of two eternities, the past and future, which is precisely the present moment; to toe that line.

We sleep, and at length awake to the still reality of a winter morning. The snow lies warm as cotton or down upon the window-sill; the broadened sash and frosted panes admit a dim and private light, which enhances the snug cheer within. The stillness of the morning is impressive. . . . From the eaves and fences hang stalactites of snow, and in the yard stand stalagmites covering some concealed core. The trees and shrubs rear white arms to the sky on every side; and where were walls and fences we see fantastic forms stretching in the frolic gambols across the dusky landscape, as if nature had strewn her fresh designs over the fields by night as models for man's art.

The finest workers in stone are not copper or steel tools, but the gentle touches of air and water working at their leisure with a liberal allowance of time.

A man who has at length found something to do will not need to get a new suit to do it in; for him the old will do, that has lain dusty in the garret for an indeterminate period. Old shoes will serve a hero longer than they have served his valet,—if a hero ever has a valet,—bare feet are older than shoes, and he can make them do. Only they who go to soirées and legislative halls must have new coats, coats to change as often as the man changes in them. But if my jacket and trousers, my hat and shoes, are fit to worship God in, they will do; will they not?

The sky appears broader now than it did. The day has opened its eyelids wider. The lengthening of the days, commenced a good while ago, is a kind of forerunner of spring.

While I enjoy the friendship of the seasons I trust that nothing can make life a burden to me. The gentle rain which waters my beans and keeps me in the house to-day is not drear and melancholy, but good for me too.

Though it prevents my hoeing them, it is of far more worth than my hoeing. If it should continue so long as to cause the seeds to rot in the ground and destroy the potatoes in the low lands, it would still be good for the grass on the uplands, and, being good for the grass, it would be good for me.

We are hunters pursing the summer on snowshoes and skates, all winter long. There is really but one season in our hearts.

As long as I have the friendship of the seasons life will never be a burden to me.

CHAPTER 4

WHAT REALLY MATTERS

Thoreau on Nature is of course also Thoreau on human nature and on the priorities for him and the false gods he sees everywhere. Emerson wrote, "He wanted a fallacy to expose, a blunder to pillory." He needed a "roll of the drum" to bring forth his full effort: "It cost him nothing to say No; indeed, he found it much easier than to say Yes." In public, this could be chilling. One friend said: "I love Henry but I cannot like him; and as for taking his arm, I should as soon think of taking the arm of an elm-tree."

His principles were hard-won and steely. What really mattered to him he outlined with stunning clarity in the second chapter of *Walden*. He wanted to be a human being who was fully alive, alert to the possibilities of life, wise to the ways in which life can be spoiled by hurry and waste.

He is too severe for our time—claiming that there is no need for railroads, that all news is repetitive and unworthy of notice—whether of a man whose eyes have been gouged out on the Wacito River or that one mad dog has been killed, or a plague of grasshoppers has come one winter. But his principles are sound: our lives are "frittered away" by what is inconsequential; an "alluvium" of habit and opinion; "prejudice, and tradition, and delusion, and appearance" cover everything and he wants a

"Realometer" to tell how far he has to dig to get to "reality." We need not go all the way with Thoreau, but a bit less comfort food and entertainment—and a lot more wisdom—will help us to understand what really matters.

It's not what you're looking at that matters, it's what you see.

Many men go fishing all of their lives without knowing that it is not fish they are after.

Wealth is the ability to fully experience life.

Superfluous wealth can buy superfluities only. Money is not required to buy one necessary of the soul.

Men of profit increase the ordinary decay of nature.

That man is rich whose pleasures are the cheapest.

Rather than love, than money, than fame, give me truth.

O how I laugh when I think of my vague indefinite riches. No run on my bank can drain it, for my wealth is not possession but enjoyment.

You did not invent it; it was imposed on you. Examine your authority.

Nature will bear the closest inspection. She invites us to lay our eye level with her smallest leaf, and take an insect view of its plain.

I have learned, that if one advances confidently in the direction of his dreams, and endeavors to live the life he has imagined, he will meet with a success unexpected in common hours.

If a man walks in the woods for love of them half of each day, he is in danger of being regarded as a loafer. But if he spends his days as a speculator, shearing off those woods and making the earth bald before her time, he is deemed an industrious and enterprising citizen.

Most of the luxuries, and many of the so-called comforts of life, are not only dispensable, but positive hindrances to the elevation of mankind. With respect to luxuries and comforts, the wisest have ever lived a more simple and meager life than the poor. The ancient philosophers, Chinese, Hindoo, Persian, and Greek, were a class which none has been poorer in outward riches, none so rich in inward. . . . The same is true of the more modern reformers and benefactors of their race. None can be an impartial or wise observer of human life but from the vantage ground of what *we* should call voluntary poverty.

Our life is frittered away by detail . . . simplify, simplify.

Sweep away the clutter of things that complicate our lives.

Our inventions are wont to be pretty toys, which distract our attention from serious things. They are but improved means to an unimproved end.

Why should we be in such desperate haste to succeed, and in such desperate enterprises? If a man does not keep pace with his companions, perhaps it is because he hears a different drummer.

One day when I went out to my wood-pile, or rather my pile of stumps, I observed two large ants, the one red, the other much larger, nearly half an inch long, and black, fiercely contending with one another. Having once got hold they never let go, but struggled and wrestled and rolled on the chips incessantly. Looking farther, I was surprised to find that the chips were covered with such combatants, that it was not a duellum, but a bellum, a war between two races of ants, the red always pitted against the black, and frequently two red ones to one black. . . . On every side they were engaged in deadly combat, yet without any noise that I could hear, and human soldiers never fought so resolutely.

Time is but the stream I go fishing in. I drink at it, but while I drink I see the sandy bottom and detect how shallow it is. Its thin current slides away, but eternity remains.

As you simplify your life, the laws of the universe will be simpler; solitude will not be solitude, poverty will not be poverty, nor weakness weakness.

I had often stood on the banks of the Concord, watching the lapse of the current, an emblem of all progress, following the same law with the system, with time, and all that is made; the weeds at the bottom gently bending down the stream, shaken by the watery wind, still planted where their seeds had sunk, but ere long to die and go down likewise; the shining pebbles, not yet anxious to better their condition, the chips and weeds, and occasional logs and stems of trees, that floated past, fulfilling their fate, were objects of singular interest to me, and at last I resolved to launch myself on its bosom, and float whither it would bear me.

It is remarkable how long men will believe in the bottomlessness of a pond without taking the trouble to sound it.

CHAPTER 5

PINE TREES OVER PEOPLE

The argument can surely be made that Thoreau is a friend to the pine tree and the fox and certainly an enemy of the state. He says, in "Civil Disobedience," that the Jeffersonian motto about a government being best that governs least in his vision should be that the best government is the one that governs not at all. He loves the natural world and is genuinely repelled by the way the humanity around him is chiefly not fully human.

He loves to be alone. He says he has "my own sun and moon and stars, and a little world all to myself." He thrills to the fact that "There can be no very black melancholy to him who lives in the midst of nature and has his senses still."

In *Walden's* "Solitude" he explores what it means to live alone, particularly in nature. "I have never felt lonesome," he announces. He speaks of the "sweet and beneficent society in nature," pleasant hours during a long rainstorm, listening to the laughing of a loon. And he asks, more metaphysically, "Shall I not have intelligence with the earth? Am I not partly leaves and vegetable mould myself?"

Still, this is a dilemma for the modern reader of Thoreau. Even if we live in a great city with all of its unique signs, sounds, and challenges, can we harness the spirit of solitude and, like Thoreau, harness the joy it can bring, wherever we happen to be?

I had three chairs in my house; one for solitude, two for friendship, three for society.

Nothing makes the earth seem so spacious as to have friends at a distance; they make the latitudes and longitudes.

My nearest neighbor is a mile distant, and no house is visible from any place but the hill-tops within half a mile of my own. I have my horizon bounded by woods all to myself; a distant view of the railroad where it touches the pond on the one hand, and of the fence which skirts the woodland road on the other.

I have never found a companion that was so companionable as solitude. We are for the most part more lonely when we go abroad among men than when we stay in our chambers. A man thinking or working is always alone, let him be where he will.

I have, as it were, my own sun and moon and stars, and a little world all to myself.

The most I can do for my friend is simply be his friend.

I would rather sit on a pumpkin, and have it all to myself, than be crowded on a velvet cushion.

Thank God men cannot fly, and lay waste the sky as well as the earth.

To be awake is to be alive. I have never yet met a man who was quite awake. How could I have looked him in the face?

The language of friendship is not words but meanings.

The finest qualities of our nature, like the bloom on fruits, can be preserved only by the most delicate handling. Yet we do not treat ourselves nor one another thus tenderly.

Of what use the friendliest disposition even, if there are no hours given to Friendship, if it is forever postponed to unimportant duties and relations? Friendship first, Friendship last.

I went to the woods because I wished to live deliberately, to front only the essential facts of life, and see if I could not learn what it had to teach, and not, when I came to die, discover that I had not lived. I did not wish to live what was not life, living is so dear; nor did I wish to practise resignation, unless it was quite necessary. I wanted to live deep and suck out all the marrow of life, to live so sturdily and Spartan-like as to put to rout all that was not life, to cut a broad swath and shave close, to drive life into a corner, and reduce it to its lowest terms.

I have never felt lonesome, or in the least oppressed by a sense of solitude, but once, and that was a few weeks after I came to the woods, when, for an hour, I doubted if the near neighborhood of man was not essential to a serene and healthy life. To be alone was something unpleasant. But I was at the same time conscious of a slight insanity in my mood, and seemed to foresee my recovery.

I have a great deal of company in my house; especially in the morning, when nobody calls.

Society is commonly too cheap. We meet at very short intervals, not having had time to acquire any new value for each other. We meet at meals three times a day, and give each other a new taste of that musty old cheese that we are. We have had to agree on a certain set of rules, called etiquette and politeness, to make this frequent meeting tolerable and that we need not come to open war. We meet at the post office, and at the sociable, and at the fireside every night; we live thick and are in each other's way, and stumble over one another, and I think that we thus lose some respect for one another.

The finest qualities of our nature, like the bloom on fruits, can be preserved only by the most delicate handling. Yet we do not treat ourselves nor one another thus tenderly.

Solitude is not measured by the miles of space that intervene between a man and his fellows. The really diligent student in one of the crowded hives of Cambridge College is as solitary as a dervis in the desert.

Even the utmost good-will and harmony and practical kindness are not sufficient for Friendship, for Friends do not live in harmony merely, as some say, but in melody. We do not wish for Friends to feed and clothe our bodies—neighbors are kind enough for that—but to do the like office to our spirits.

In the midst of a gentle rain while these thoughts prevailed, I was suddenly sensible of such sweet and beneficent society in Nature, in the very pattering of the drops, and in every sound and sight around my house, an infinite and unaccountable friendliness all at once, like an atmosphere sustaining me, as made the fancied advantages of human neighborhood insignificant, and I have never thought of them since. Every little pine needle expanded and swelled with sympathy and befriended me.

CHAPTER 6

LIVING WITH THE LAND

"In wildness is the preservation of the world" was Thoreau's motto. But the small log cabin he built at Walden Pond wasn't in the middle of the woods, secreted from civilization. Rather, he built his famous dwelling on the outskirts of Concord, Massachusetts. He did not need to live completely off the land but his two-mile sojourn was carried out with a cheerful desire to make his life of "equal simplicity" with Nature.

"Simplicity" is the key. He wanted to live with the rhythms of the day and the season, with the produce of his simple garden, and with as much time as possible to see and experience the lessons Nature teaches.

In the "Economy" chapter of *Walden*, Thoreau writes: "Near the end of March, 1845, I borrowed an axe and went down to the woods by Walden Pond, nearest to where I intended to build my house, and began to cut down some tall arrowy white pines." So begins his life of living with the land. He adds: "So I went on for some days cutting and hewing timber, and also studs and rafters, all with my narrow axe, not having many communicable or scholar-like thoughts, singing to myself,—

"Men say they know many things;
But lo! They have taken wings,—
The arts and sciences,
And a thousand appliances,

The wind that blows
Is all that any body knows."

This merry work is later tempered by such "brute neighbors" as warring ants and pesky woodchucks. He grows his beans in nearby fields, is awakened by squirrels and visited by wasps, and muses that in the reflection of the lake "the beholder measures the depth of his own nature." And he sets out a nuanced and compelling case for vegetarianism, as relevant today as it was then.

Just two miles beyond town limits, Thoreau carves out a self-sustaining and simple existence on the land, one that gives him freedom from the kinds of work that erode rather than refreshing and building life—allowing him to live Spartan-like and simply, hand in hand with the natural world.

My dwelling was small, and I could hardly entertain an echo in it; but it seemed larger for being a single apartment and remote from neighbors. All the attractions of a house were concentrated in one room; it was kitchen, chamber, parlor, and keeping-room; and whatever satisfaction parent or child, master or servant, derive from living in a house, I enjoyed it all.

I would observe, by the way, that it costs me nothing for curtains, for I have no gazers to shut out but the sun and moon, and I am willing that they should look in.

The wasps came by thousands to my lodge in October, as to winter quarters, and settled on my windows within and on the walls over-head, sometimes deterring visitors from entering. Each morning, when they were numbed with cold, I swept some of them out, but I did not trouble myself much to get rid of them; I even felt complimented by their regarding my house as a desirable shelter.

As drew a still fresher soil about the rows with my hoe, I disturbed the ashes of un-chronicled nations who in primeval years lived under these heavens, and their small implements of war and hunting were brought to the light of this modern day.

The fruits do not yield their true flavor to the purchaser of them, nor to him who raises them for the market. There is but one way to obtain it, yet few take it that way. If you would know the flavor of huckleberries, ask the cow-boy or the partridge.

Why concern ourselves so much about our beans for seed, and not be concerned at all about a new generation of men?

We are wont to forget that the sun looks on our cultivated fields and on the prairies and forests without distinct. They all reflect and absorb his rays alike, and the former make but a small part of the glorious picture which he beholds in his daily course. In his view the earth is all equally cultivated like a garden.

In September or October, Walden is a perfect forest mirror, set round with stones as precious to my eye as if fewer or rarer. Nothing so fair, so pure, and at the same time so large, as a lake, perchance, lies on the surface of the earth.

A lake is the landscape's most beautiful and expressive feature. It is earth's eye; looking into which the beholder measures the depth of his own nature. The fluviatile trees next the shore are the slender eyelashes which fringe it, and the wooded hills and cliffs around are its overhanging brows.

Usually the red squirrel (*Sciurus Hudsonius*) waked me in the dawn, coursing over the roof and up and down the sides of the house, as if sent out of the woods for this purpose.

I saw a muskrat come out of a hole in the ice . . . While I am looking at him, I am thinking what he is thinking of me. He is a different sort of man, that's all.

The first sparrow of spring! The year beginning with younger hope than ever!

Instead of calling on some scholar, I paid many a visit to particular trees, of kinds which are rare in this neighborhood, standing far away in the middle of some pasture, or in the depths of a wood or swamp.

If we knew all the laws of Nature, we should need only one fact, or the description of one actual phenomenon, to infer all the particular results at that point. Now we know only a few laws, and our result is vitiated, not, of course, by any confusion or irregularity in Nature, but by our ignorance of essential elements in the calculation.

After a still winter night I awoke with the impression that some question had been put to me, which I had been endeavoring in vain to answer in my sleep, as what—how—when—where? But there was dawning Nature, in whom all creatures live, looking in at my broad windows with serene and satisfied face, and no question on her lips. I awoke to an answered question, to Nature and daylight.

Once it chanced that I stood in the very abutment of a rainbow's arch, which filled

the lower stratum of the atmosphere, ting-
ing the grass and leaves around, and dazzling
me as if I looked through colored crystal.

The pond rises and falls, but whether reg-
ularly or not, and within what period, nobody knows, though, as usual, many pretend
to know.

Every morning was a cheerful invitation to
make my life of equal simplicity, and I may
say innocence, with Nature herself.

I got up early and bathed in the pond; that
was a religious exercise, and one of the best
things I did.

Nature has no human inhabitant who appre-
ciates her. The birds with their plumage and
their notes are in harmony with the flowers,
but what youth or maiden conspires with
the wild luxuriant beauty of Nature? She

flourishes most alone, far from the towns where they reside. Talk of heaven! ye disgrace earth.

One farmer says to me, 'You cannot live on vegetable food solely, for it furnishes nothing to make bones with;' and so he religiously devotes a part of his day to supplying his system with the raw material of bones; walking all the while he talks behind his oxen, which, with vegetable-made bones, jerk him and his lumbering plow along in spite of every obstacle.

He goes thither at first as a hunter and fisher, until at last, if he has the seeds of a better life in him, he distinguishes his proper objects, as a poet or naturalist it may be, and leaves the gun and fish-pole behind.

I have found repeatedly, of late years, that I cannot fish without falling a little in self-respect.

The squirrel that you kill in jest, dies in earnest.

The repugnance to animal food is not the effect of experience, but is an instinct.

I have just been through the process of killing the cistudo for the sake of science; but I cannot excuse myself for this murder, and see that such actions are inconsistent with the poetic perception, however they may serve science, and will affect the quality of my observations. I pray that I may walk more innocently and serenely through nature. No reasoning whatever reconciles me to this act. It affects my day injuriously. I have lost some self-respect. I have a murderer's experience to a degree.

Is it not a reproach that man is a carnivorous animal? True, he can and does live, in a great measure, by preying on other animals;

but this is a miserable way,—as any one who will go to snaring rabbits, or slaughter lambs, may learn,—and he will be regarded as a benefactor of his race who shall teach man to confine himself to a more innocent and wholesome diet.

I do not consider the other animals brutes in the common sense. I am attracted toward them undoubtedly because I never heard any nonsense from them. I have not convicted them of folly or vanity or pomposity or stupidity in dealing with me. Their vices, at any rate, do not interfere with me.

Whatever my own practice may be, I have no doubt that it is part of the destiny of the human race, in its gradual improvement, to leave off eating animals, as surely as the savage tribes have left off eating each other when they came in contact with the more civilized.

My enemies are worms, cool days, and most of all woodchucks.

There can be no very black melancholy to him who lives in the midst of Nature and has his senses still.

Thank God men cannot fly, and lay waste the sky as well as the earth.

We need the tonic of wildness . . . At the same time that we are earnest to explore and learn all things, we require that all things be mysterious and unexplorable, that land and sea be indefinitely wild, unsurveyed and un-fathomed by us because unfathomable. We can never have enough of nature.

CHAPTER 7

MORNING STAR

Morning may be Thoreau's predominant symbol. Morning is when he is fully awake, when "there is dawn" in him. All is possible. "Every morning," he says, "was a cheerful invitation to make my life of equal simplicity, and I may say innocence, with nature herself." He rises early and bathes in the pond. He "who does not believe that each day contains an earlier, more sacred, and auroral hour" has despaired of life.

In the clarity of a morning he can come closest to nature, see best through the "shams and delusions" in society and plot his path to an ever more intimate relationship with the natural world. "Let us spend one day as deliberately as nature," he advises, "and not be thrown off the track by every nutshell and mosquito's wing that falls on the rails. Let us rise early . . ."

Morning even when it is not morning becomes a metaphor for when he is fully awake. Close to nature he arrives in his head at an astonishing personal clarity. "The intellect," he says, "is a cleaver; it discerns and rifts its way into the secret of things. . . . My head is hands and feet," his head "is an organ for burrowing, as some creatures use their snout and fore-paws . . ."

The great joy, finally, in the writings of Henry David Thoreau on nature is the degree to which he pleads for us to live closer to the simple verities of the natural world and closer to a life that encourages our minds to be fully awake.

The surface of the earth is soft and impressible by the feet of men; and so with the paths which the mind travels. How worn and dusty, then, must be the highways of the world, how deep the ruts of tradition and conformity! I did not wish to take a cabin passage, but rather to go before the mast and on the deck of the world, for there I could best see the moonlight amid the mountains.

The morning, which is the most memorable season of the day, is the awakening hour. Then there is least somnolence in us; and for an hour, at least, some part of us awakes which slumbers all the rest of the day and night... All memorable events, I should say, transpire in morning time and in a morning atmosphere. The Vedas say, "All intelligences awake with the morning."

An early-morning walk is a blessing for the whole day.

I did not feel crowded or confined in the least. There was pasture enough for my imagination.

None are so old as those who have outlived enthusiasm.

With all your science can you tell how it is, and whence it is, that light comes into the soul?

Some of my pleasantest hours were during the long rain storms in the spring or fall, which confined me to the house for the afternoon as well as the forenoon, soothed by their ceaseless roar and pelting; when an early twilight ushered in a long evening in which many thoughts had time to take root and unfold themselves.

There is no remedy for love, but to love more.

There's nothing in the world I know
That can escape from love,
For every depth it goes below,
And every height above.

Dreams are the touchstones of our characters. Our truest life is when we are in dreams awake.

To say that God has given a man many and great talents, frequently means, that he has brought his heavens down within reach of his hands.

In all perception of the truth there is a divine ecstasy, an inexpressible delirium of joy, as when a youth embraces his betrothed virgin.

Man flows at once to God when the channel of purity is open.

Between whom there is hearty truth there is love; and in proportion to our truthfulness and confidence in one another, our lives are divine and miraculous, and answer to our ideal.

These are passages of affection that anticipate heaven for us.

This is a delicious evening, when the whole body is one sense, and imbibes delight through every pore. I go and come with strange liberty in Nature, a part of herself.

The mass of men lead lives of quiet desperation. What is called resignation is confirmed desperation. From the desperate city you go into the desperate country, and have to console yourself with the bravery of minks and muskrats. A stereotyped but unconscious despair is concealed even under what are called the games and amusements of mankind. There is no play in them, for this comes after work. But it is a characteristic of wisdom not to do desperate things.

As I walk through the stony shore of the pond in my shirt sleeves, though it is cool as well as cloudy and windy, and I see nothing to attract me, all the elements are unusually congenial to me.

I once had a sparrow alight upon my shoulder for a moment, while I was hoeing in a village garden, and I felt that I was more distinguished by that circumstance than I should have been by any epaulet I could have worn.

My profession is always to be alert, to find God in nature, to know God's lurking places, to attend to all the oratorios and the operas in nature.

Love must be as much a light as it is a flame.

Though I do not believe that a plant will spring up where no seed has been, I have great faith in a seed. Convince me that you have a seed there, and I am prepared to expect wonders.

Happiness is like a butterfly; the more you chase it, the more it will elude you, but if you turn your attention to other things, it will come and sit softly on your shoulder.

Heaven is under our feet as well as over our heads.

Morning is when I am awake and there is a dawn in me.

To be awake is to be alive.

The imagination, give it the least license, dives deeper and soars higher than Nature goes.

If a plant cannot live according to its nature, it dies; and so a man.

Sympathy with the fluttering alder and poplar leaves almost takes away my breath; yet, like the lake, my serenity is rippled but not ruffled.

He who hears the rippling of rivers in these degenerate days will not utterly despair.

If the day and night are such that you greet them with joy, and life emits a fragrance like flowers and sweet-scented herbs, is more elastic, more starry, more immortal - that is your success.

I found in myself, and still find, an instinct toward a higher, or, as it is named, spiritual life, as do most men, and another toward a primitive rank and savage one, and I reverence them both. I love the wild not less than the good.

May we not *see* God? Are we to be put off and amused in this life, as it were with a mere allegory? Is not Nature, rightly read, that of which she is commonly taken to be the symbol merely? When the common man looks into the sky, which he has not so much profaned, he thinks it less gross than the earth, and with reverence speaks of "the Heavens," but the seer will in the same sense speak of "the Earths" and his Father who is in them. "Did not he that made that which is *within*, make that which is *without* also?"

I believe that men are generally still a little afraid of the dark, though the witches are all hung, and Christianity and candles have been introduced. Yet I experienced sometimes that the most sweet and tender, the most innocent and encouraging society may be found in any natural object, even for the poor misanthrope and melancholy man. There can be no very black melancholy to him who lives in the midst of Nature and has his senses still.

The world is but a canvas to the imagination.

The light which puts out our eyes is darkness to us. Only that day dawns to which we are awake. There is more day to dawn. The sun is but a morning star.

I hear beyond the range of sound,
I see beyond the range of sight,
New earths and skies and seas around,
And in my day the sun doth pale his light.
All good things are wild and free.

BIBLIOGRAPHY

Emerson, Ralph Waldo. *The Complete Works of Ralph Waldo Emerson (Unexpurgated Edition)*. Houston, Texas: Halcyon Press, 2009.

Hodder, Alan D. *Thoreau's Ecstatic Witness*. New Haven, Connecticut: Yale University Press, 2001.

Meltzer, Milton and Walter Harding. *A Thoreau Profile* (reissue edition). Thoreau Society, 1998.

Thoreau, Henry David. *Collected Essays and Poems*. Library of America, 2001.

Thoreau, Henry David and Franklin Benjamin Sanborn. *Familiar Letters*. Bibliolife, 2008.

Thoreau, Henry David. *Life Without Principle.* Forgotten Books, 2008.

Thoreau, Henry David. *Walden* (1854). Philadelphia: The Franklin Library, 1983.

Thoreau, Henry David. *A Week on the Concord and Merrimack Rivers.* Boston: Houghton Mifflin, 1906.